CRYING FOR A VISION

A ROSEBUD SIOUX TRILOGY 1886·1976

Photographs by

John A. Anderson,

Eugene Buechel, S.J.

Don Doll, S.J.

Edited by

Don Doll, S.J. and Jim Alinder

Foreword by

Ben Black Bear, Jr.

Introduction by

Herman Viola

MORGAN & MORGAN

1976

This book was made possible through the cooperation of the
Mid-America Arts Alliance headquartered in Kansas City, Missouri.
The M-AAA is a regional partnership of the Office of Arkansas State
Arts and Humanities, the Kansas Arts Commission, the Missouri Arts
Council, the Nebraska Arts Council, and the Oklahoma Arts and
Humanities Council.

The touring exhibition on which this book is based was made possible
through regional support and grants from the National Endowment
for the Arts, a Federal Agency.

Exhibit and book coordinated by Henry Moran and David L. Smith.

Book design by David Laufer
Typeset in Goudy Old Style
Originally printed in Quadradot Lithography
by Morgan Press Incorporated

Morgan & Morgan, Inc.
Publishers
145 Palisade Street
Dobbs Ferry, New York 10522

International Standard Book Number 0-87100-104-7
Library of Congress Catalogue Card Number 76-25392

Printed and bound in Hong Kong

Second Printing 1991

Preface

During the summer of 1975, three independent but compatible projects were brought to the attention of the Mid-American Arts Alliance. Through research at the Nebraska State Historical Society, Jim Alinder, professor of photography at the University of Nebraska, and David Smith of the M-AAA staff, became familiar with the Rosebud Sioux Reservation photographs by John A. Anderson made at the turn of the century. Through professional contacts Alinder was also aware of Rosebud photographs by Eugene Buechel, S.J., made in the 1920's through 40's. Creighton University professor Don Doll, S.J., presented an exhibition in Omaha of his photographs reflecting upon contemporary life of the Brule Sioux. Jim Alinder then suggested a Rosebud photographic trilogy.

The M-AAA, dedicated to presenting quality programs with indigenous visual arts resources, realized the opportunity that presented itself for an original exhibition bringing forth a unique statement from essentially unknown sources; viewed together, the visual records portrayed a people's cultural transformation over nearly a century of Indian reservation life. An interesting sidelight was the fact that the three photographers involved first started to photograph when living on the Reservation.

Jim Alinder and Don Doll were invited to participate as co-curators for the exhibition and subsequently agreed to become co-editors for this book and exhibition catalogue.

From the beginning we established two basic guidelines as our parameters. First, we would work closely with the people of the Rosebud regarding content and statement, particularly because we were dealing with a subject of recent public attention, growing social concern and great sensitivity. Secondly, we would utilize Don Doll's previously presented sequence and statement — the Land, the People and the Quality of Life.

Of the thousands of glass plates John Anderson made less than 400 remain. From the archives at the Nebraska State Historical Society, Jim Alinder made an initial selection. From nearly 2000 Buechel negatives, stored at the Buechel Memorial Lakota Museum on the Rosebud Reservation, Don Doll selected and processed a preliminary choice. He also began editing his own photographs. Slowly they narrowed their recommendations to 40 prints from each photographer. They were sent to M-AAA and the Rosebud for discussion and concurrence on their inclusion. Jim Alinder made exhibition prints of the Anderson and Buechel plates and negatives and Father Doll printed his own work.

For the exhibition the photographs stand on their own. Yet in developing this book we were inclined toward the advantages of text. We sought copy original to the photographers that could augment our perception of their consideration and attitudes toward their subject. However, research did not uncover commentary directly from either Anderson or Buechel on their images. For Buechel's photographs we have provided some brief excerpts from his personal correspondence. Perhaps sufficiently revealing about Anderson is a statement attributed to him and his wife in their booklet *Sioux Memory Gems*

We are only trying to make known the fact that God breathed into the Indian a soul of which the public at large knows little nor has ever tried to understand.

And, with Doll's photographs we are giving his own commentary. These images comprise a subjective chronicle on the Brule Sioux during a long century of American life. The title, *Crying For A Vision* is Black Elk's translation of *Hanblecheyapi* the ritual of the vision quest at the center of the Sioux Indian religion. Black Elk explained that visions "help us to realize our oneness with all things, to know that all things are relatives."

Henry Moran
David L. Smith

Acknowledgements

The unity of effort creating this project is significant.

We are indebted to the Nebraska State Historical Society and its Director, Marvin F. Kivett, for the use of the John A. Anderson glass negatives for reproduction; with special thanks to their staff members, Ann Reinert, Opal Jacobson and Carol Callahan.

We are deeply appreciative of the cooperation, concern and guidance provided by the Buechel Memorial Lakota Museum, St. Francis, South Dakota, and Director, Harold Moore, for use of the Eugene J. Buechel, S.J., photographic archives. We extend our sincere appreciation to their Board, particularly Victor Douville, Chairman, Ben Black Bear, Jr., whose foreword is contained herein, and the assuring direction of Father Bernard Fagan, S.J., Director of the St. Francis Mission.

We are pleased that Don Doll, S.J., Creighton University, is represented as artist and thank him for his editorial contribution. Our thanks as well go to Creighton's Michael Flecky, S.J., for his biographies on the three photographers.

The continued leadership of the University of Nebraska in our region is profound. Jim Alinder's patience and skill as co-editor and printer of the Anderson and Buechel materials, and unselfish assistance throughout the project was motivating to us all. Director Norman Geske, and Assistant Jon Nelson of the University's Sheldon Memorial Art Gallery lent us their unmeasurable support and provided the facilities to assemble both meetings of the minds and the touring exhibition. Additionally noteworthy is the advocacy from University of Nebraska President and M-AAA Chairman, D. B. Varner.

We are also deeply appreciative of Dr. Herman J. Viola, Director of the National Anthropological Archives, Museum of Natural History, Smithsonian Institution, who wrote and contributed the introduction.

We must surely recognize: The State Arts Agencies comprising M-AAA, and especially their directors, Jonathan Katz, Gerald L. Ness, Bill Jamison, Dr. Sandra Perry, Emily Rice and John Amberg for their constant leadership and cooperative support exemplifying what M-AAA is all about; Charlotte Carver, Director of the South Dakota Fine Arts Council for her continued encouragement; the National Endowment for the Arts and its Visual Arts Office; the M-AAA Board and staff, most especially Claire Rupard, Will Conner and David Smith, whose dedicated and continued commitment make it all possible.

Henry Moran

Foreword

*Written in his native tongue, Lakota,
and literally translated, by*
Ben Black Bear, Jr.

Ehanni Lakota ki okaśpeśpeya wico'un ki hena iyohila wicaśa eya wicayuhapi. Lena wicaśa ki waniyetu yawapi kaġa pi ca lena oyate ki wicegna un pi. Lena wicaśa ki inś'eya wicaśa itacan iyecel wicayu'onihanpi na wicaśa tanka heca pi. Lena wicaśa ki ehank'ehan wico'un wan hehan waniyetu iyohi oyate ki taku ecun pi na akipa pi ki hena iyuha kiksuya un pi. Anpetu wan el wicaśa itacan ki ob iyotaka pi na waniyetu opta taku wokiksuye tankinkinyan ki hena iyuha iwoglaka pi na ho le wanji kahniġa pi. Wanji kahniġa pi ki le waniyetu yawa pi kage ki le icu na tahalo wan akan waniyetu yawa pi kage ki hel owa. Ho le tohancin ki oyate ki wokiksuye yuha pi, na he un hektakiya oyate ki u pun he wankiglaka pi na slolkiya pi. Ca lena wicaśa ki wowaśi wan lila tanka ca ecun pi.

Wicaśa ki lena wicaśa waśte heca pi. Iglu'onihan pi, na wacantognaka pi, na wicaśa ki ksapa pi. Oyate ki toske wiyukcan pi na toske tawacin pi ki lena wicasa ki lena slolya un pi. Ho hece ins'eya wicaśa itacan pi ki wa'iyehanyan najin pi, ob wa'akilehanyan un pi. Lena wicaśa ki wo'unspe wan yuha pi na he eca un oyate ki wawokiya pi. Oyate to'un ki tohancin ki hektakiya yapi ki hena kiksuye wicakiya pi na hena slolya un pi. Hecel oyate ki han tokiyatanhan upi na toske le omaka el hinajin pi ki hena slolkiya pi kte.

Wowapi ki le ins'eya waniyetu yawa pi ki he iyecel wopazo heca. Hektakiya waniyetu wikcemna sakowin wahecetuya oyate ki Sicanġu Oyanke ki lel tokeske un pi heci he eca pazo. Itowapi un lena wowanyanke ki kaga pi. Wicaśa yamni wicitowa ki lena icupi. Lena wicaśa ki ins'eya ehank'ehan waniyetu yawa pi kaga pi k'un hena iyecel Lakota oyate pi ki wicegna un pi na oyate ki tokeske un pun he iyecel ins'eya ni un pi, oyate ki tokel wiyukcan pi na tokel tawacin pun hena slolya na wanyang un pi. Lecel oyate ki slolwicaya pi ki he un ca itowapi ki lena kaga pi. Na le anpetu ki el itowapi ki lena un wowapi kaga pi na maga sitomniyan Lakota ki toske unk'un pun he owicakiyaka pi cin pi un lena pazo pi kte. Ca wowapi ki le Lakota tawokiksuye heca, na he unkitan pi kta iyececa.

In the early days when the Lakota people lived in groups, each group had a man among them who was to be the tribal historian. These men were the makers of the winter count and they lived among the people. These men were respected by the people as the leaders of the tribe were, and they were also usually elders of the tribe. These men in the prereservation period were the ones who kept a mental record of all that happened to the people throughout the past year and remembered these for the people. On a particular day in summer they would sit down with the other leaders of the tribe and talk about the important happenings during the past year. At the end they came up with one event which was considered by the majority of the people as the most important event of the year. This event was then taken by the keeper of the winter count and put on a buffalo hide on which he kept the winter count. The people then would have a recorded account of their past events, and they could see and understand how they had lived and progressed over the years.

The keeper of the winter count was a good man. He was a man of honor, one who practiced generosity, and above all he was a man of wisdom. He had a good understanding of the people and knew their innermost thoughts, because he lived as they did. He was considered equal in every respect to the other leaders of the tribe, since he knew all about the people. This man possessed a skill which he used for the benefit of the whole tribe. He kept a history of the people for their remembrance as far back as history could record it. Thus the people would have a good understanding of their origins and early history and understand how they arrived at the place where they were in the present. The winter count was a proud achievement of the Lakota people.

This book is also to the Lakota an achievement similar to the winter count. It is a photographic record of the life of the Lakota people for more or less seventy years of reservation life. The telling of the story of the people is done with photographs. The photographs were done by three men. These three men lived among the people, lived as they did, and got to know the thoughts and attitudes of the people. These men took photographs of the people based on the knowledge and identity they had with the people. They felt a need to preserve the memory of the Lakota in photographic form in such a way that the photographs will tell a story. Today these photographs have been taken and made into book form so that the story of the Lakota can be told nationwide. This book is a winter count in modern day form that tells the story of our past and we should be proud of it.

Introduction

by Herman J. Viola, *Director*
National Anthropological Archives
National Museum of Natural History
Smithsonian Institution

Perhaps no aspect of the American West has captured the popular imagination more than the image of warbonneted Indian warriors astride splendid ponies, sweeping across the prairies in pursuit of adventure. To most of us, the Plains Indians symbolize all Indians, and none are more romantic than the Sioux, who fought hard and well to protect their traditional way of life. Their wonderful resistance to white encroachment has made places like the Little Bighorn and Wounded Knee as much a part of our American heritage as the Alamo and Sutter's Mill. But the brutal and bloody struggle left the Sioux an embittered people living in economic poverty and under great cultural stress upon barren isolated reservations. Where once they roamed freely across the northern plains, they were now forced to accept a way of life they neither wanted nor understood.

Our society continues to foster the image of an Indian way of life that experienced traumatic disruptions almost a century ago. The stereotypes die hard because most of us have little contact with Indians except through photographs and an occasional motion picture documentary. Even these are often simplistic views of Indians garbed in ceremonial dress and participating in parades or powwows that do little more than perpetuate the existing stereotypes. Seldom is there a candid, sensitive portrayal of reservation life as it really exists—the isolation, the boredom, the frustration, the poverty—because it is a side of Indian life that is harsh and unattractive. That is why this pictorial essay of the Brule Sioux is so unique and important.

The Brule, or Burnt Thigh, Sioux belong to the Teton division of the great Dakota tribe, one of the most numerous tribal groups in early history of North America. The Brule apparently acquired their name from an incident that occurred in the middle of the eighteenth century when they were migrating with the other Teton Sioux bands from their earlier homelands on the upper reaches of the Mississippi River to their present location west of the Missouri, where Lewis and Clark met them in 1804. The band was encamped one night along the shore of a South Dakota lake when a prairie fire engulfed the village. Most of the Sioux saved themselves by leaping into the water, although many suffered bad burns on their legs and thighs. Thereafter, French traders, wishing to distinguish them from other Sioux bands, called them the Brule.

The Brule were skilled horsemen and warriors, and, for more than a century, they enjoyed the typical life of the Northern Plains

Indians. They retained their independence until the disappearance of the buffalo and white pressure forced them to give up their nomadic ways. Thanks to the able leadership of Sinte Gleska and other Brule headmen, the majority of Brule managed to be steered to a course of neutrality when faced with the overwhelming pressure of white encroachments, but still tenaciously struggling against these injustices by talks, agreements and trips to Washington.

In 1868, the Brule agreed to the Fort Laramie treaty, which theoretically provided a permanent reservation for the various Sioux bands and many benefits including schools, tools, and instruction in agriculture. Almost ten years passed, however, before the Spotted Tail or Rosebud Agency was established. Although Spotted Tail led his people onto the reservation in November 1877, the Brule continually resisted government efforts to make them farmers. Instead, they have clung tenaciously to the surviving vestiges of their traditional culture, including numerous religious ceremonies and their language which is still widely spoken throughout the reservation.

Crying For a Vision documents the Brule Sioux's adjustment to reservation life. That the transition was not easy can be seen from the photographs by John Anderson, which reflect his awareness that he was observing a unique phenomenon that should be recorded for posterity. Here are people caught between two worlds. Metal pots and pans are used alongside hide containers. Wagons are common, but the travois is still evident. Clothing is a fantastic array of buckskins, blankets, cowboy hats, and machine-made dresses. Canvas tipis are grudgingly giving way to cabins, but some Brule families have both. Each homestead also boasts a veteran or two of the Indian wars, and these aging but proud warriors need little encouragement to don the badges of honor they earned on the battlefields of another era. The buffalo are gone, so the white man's cattle are slaughtered from horseback until officials in Washington decide it is time to end this sad parody of a former way of life.

Father Buechel continued the pictorial narrative through both World Wars. His invaluable photographs document Brule Sioux life in an era when they, like most reservation Indians, were literally a forgotten people. During Anderson's time, most observers believed in the concept of the "Vanishing Red Man", and the Indians did vanish in a sense because once settled on their reservations, they were out of sight and out of mind. Ironically, it was in this period that the Indians, as so well expressed in these photographs, tried earnestly and painfully to become white. Note the close cropped hair, the store-bought clothes, the absence of blankets and feathers. The Brule Sioux, like their brethren elsewhere, were trying to emulate life in mainstream America. As for their own culture, it may have deteriorated, but it was not destroyed. Threads of Brule Sioux traditional life survived to be reawakened in the cultural resurgence of recent years.

Major changes occurred in Brule life because of the World Wars, particularly World War II when so many Indian men left the reservation to fight for a country they were not quite a part of. Their patriotism is remarkable and quite evident from the flags and other similar symbols that abound in the photographs. True, in the militarism of the United States the Sioux found an outlet for their warrior tradition, but it is equally true that they have a genuine regard for their country that others in American society would do well to emulate.

Father Doll's photographs are an excellent portrayal of contemporary Brule life. They reveal a great empathy between the photographer and his subjects. His photographs also reveal an attempt on the part of the Brule to return to lost values. Young men once again wear their hair long. Even feathers are evident. They are proud to be Indians, and they no longer attempt to conceal that fact.

Perhaps it is sadly appropriate that this portfolio concludes with a funeral procession, for it is still only through drink and death that some of the Brule Sioux can escape the boredom, isolation, and poverty that remain so much a part of their lives.

Certain other themes also persist to the present. The horse remains an important symbol of freedom, strength, and wealth, although the motorcycle and automobile are now the basic means of transportation. Guns and violence play a small part of Brule life, and there is a little air of militancy and defiance.

Nevertheless, for the most part, the Brule are no different from Americans everywhere. They work, they play, they dream, they have to cope with the pressures of an increasingly complex and fast paced society. Reservation life may be improving, but much remains to be done. The Brule Sioux are indeed a people crying for a vision.

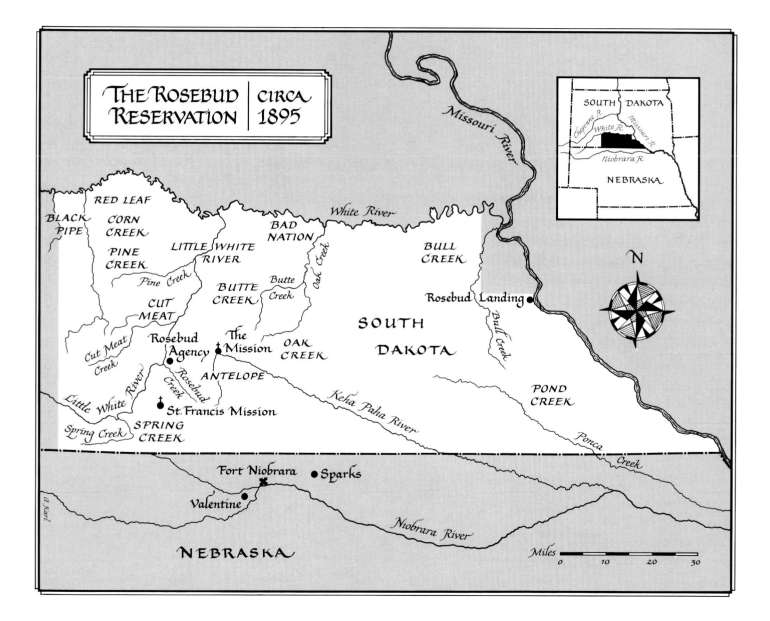

THE ROSEBUD RESERVATION | CIRCA 1895

SOUTH DAKOTA

Missouri River

White River

RED LEAF

BLACK PIPE

CORN CREEK

PINE CREEK

LITTLE WHITE RIVER

Pine Creek

BAD NATION

BULL CREEK

Oak Creek

BUTTE CREEK

Butte Creek

Rosebud Landing

CUT MEAT

Cut Meat Creek

SOUTH DAKOTA

N

Rosebud Agency

The Mission

OAK CREEK

Little White River

Rosebud Creek

ANTELOPE

POND CREEK

St. Francis Mission

Keha Paha River

Spring Creek

SPRING CREEK

Bull Creek

Ponca Creek

Fort Niobrara

Sparks

Valentine

a. Karl

Niobrara River

NEBRASKA

Miles
0   10   20   30

NEBRASKA

The Photographers

Seven years before the Wounded Knee massacre, John A. Anderson arrived as a teenager in the Rosebud area. He began his career as a photographer there two years later in 1885, using a view camera and glass plates, usually 8x10 inches. The slow emulsion plates required his subjects to be posed.

Anderson is at his best in the formal portraits of the Sioux. His direct technique and plain background eliminate all but the essential and thrust forward the character of these people. When Anderson acquired a scenic studio backdrop, popular at the turn of the century, the inevitable posing of the Sioux in front of it presents us with an ironic cultural warp.

Anderson took care to photograph the daily life on the reservation and posed reasonable facsimiles where he was not able to photograph the actual situation. The extreme of this "set-up" is his *Sioux Sportsmen* — a post card reality for romanticizing by the rest of the world.

Eugene J. Buechel, S.J., photographed the Rosebud from 1922 to 1945 while serving as a priest on the reservation. He used the simplest of adjustable cameras, a folding Kodak No. 3, had his film developed commercially and apparently neither knew nor cared about the photographic process. Appropriately, Buechel's photographs have the stylistic directness of snapshots. Only in the past decade has this naive, direct approach to photography been recognized as a legitimate art form. Buechel's clarity of statement is not camouflaged by sophisticated technique.

Buechel made many of his photographs as records of an event and gave prints to the subjects. In the photograph of the marriage of Joe Understanding Crow and Melissa Holy Eagle the couple look directly at the photographer, not at us. They are photographed straight-on without careful posing. Clearly there is a warm rapport evident in all the Buechel portraits. Other of his photographs document the quality of reservation life from the cooking of meals to tribal ceremonies to religious observances.

While Don Doll, S.J., lived on the Rosebud during the mid-1960's as a young Jesuit teacher, these photographs were made since 1974 when Doll spent an extended time photographing the Spring Creek community on Rosebud.

Now we move from the sunlit outdoor photographs of Anderson and Buechel to the interiors of the Sioux homes. With his Leica and fast film, Doll has photographed the people in their environment and has given us a humanistic vision of reservation life today.

We can enjoy the grandeur presented in the Anderson photographs, and can all too easily pass off the Buechel pictures as life in the difficult years of the Great Depression, but the disquieting situation described in the photographs of Doll present us with people living and dying now.

If we trace a visual history from Anderson's *Fool Bull* through Buechel's *Arthur White Feather and His Wife, Nellie Running,* to Doll's *Sewel Makes Room For Them,* we see a dramatic evolution. As pervasive as reservation problems are, the strong character of the Brule Sioux permeates these photographs. Brought together, these three concerned photographers give us much of the information necessary for our own understanding and decisions.

Jim Alinder

John A. Anderson

arrived in Rosebud country in 1883 at the age of 14. His family had immigrated to Pennsylvania from Stockholm, Sweden, where John was born on March 25, 1869. He accompanied his father and three brothers on the trip from Pennsylvania to the west, settling in the area near Fort Niobrara and the present town of Valentine, Nebraska. John became immediately engaged in constructing the Anderson homestead in Cherry County and supplementing the family income by carpentry work in Valentine. Within two years he had saved the money to buy his first camera, an 8x10 Primo viewcamera with revolving back. By 1885, at the age of 16, he had begun his serious photographic career with his first commission as a civilian photographer with the Army at Fort Niobrara.

In the ensuing years Anderson photographed widely in Rosebud country for the Army and equipped a commercial studio at Fort Niobrara for his own enterprises. Most of his earliest photographs were made as commercial requests from the soldiers at the fort or as official documentation of their wide-ranging movements in the field. His most significant early contact with the Rosebud Sioux was in the capacity of official photographer during the negotiations of the Crook Treaty Commission in 1889. He seemingly enjoyed the trust and friendship of the Sioux almost immediately and the success of his early contacts provided the basis for a later personal and photographic rapport with the Sioux that was exceptional.

Anderson discontinued his commercial studio at Fort Niobrara and his work for the Army precisely one year before the tragedy at Wounded Knee. Between 1890 and 1895 Anderson made three trips back to Pennsylvania, continued commercial photographic work in Valentine, and began work as a clerk for the Jordan Trading Post at the Rosebud Agency. On his last return from Pennsylvania he was accompanied by his bride, Myrtle Miller. They settled in Rosebud where John had by now acquired an interest in the Jordan Trading Post and where they would reside for the next forty-two years.

It was during the period after 1895 and before 1915 that John Anderson's most significant photographs of the Rosebud Sioux were made. He abandoned his earlier landscape technique and concentrated on formal studio portraits or family portraits in a local outdoor setting. These photographs include the best and perhaps the only existing images of the great Rosebud chiefs and important families. They are both photographically impressive and historically monumental records of a past life revered in the memory and consciousness of the Rosebud Sioux.

In 1936 John and Myrtle Anderson moved to Rapid City, South Dakota, where John developed and managed the Sioux Indian Museum for three years. They later moved permanently to Atascadero, California, where John died of cancer June 26, 1948. Only within the past 25 years have the scattered prints, existing plates and sketchy diaries of John Anderson enjoyed the attention they deserve among photographers and historians.

Rosebud Agency, 1889

Crow Dog, circa 1898

Chief Two Strike, 1896

Watering horses — circa 1902

You well understand the present condition of the Indian, compared with the past. Your ability to secure a living as your father's did, is past forever. We need not talk about how this change came about. It can not be changed. A much more kindly feeling, thank God, prevails with the present 65,000,000 of American people toward our Indian brother than ever existed before. We want nothing but your good.

The Great Father and all of his people believe that your best interests will lead you, as far as you can, to adopt the habits of our civilization, and to become each and every one of you American citizens and have your share in the common glory of the country.

General Charles Foster,
Chairman, Sioux Commission, Rosebud Agency,
June 3, 1889, in addressing the Indian Council.

Chief Hollow Horn Bear, 1900

Left Hand Bull making
ceremonial arrows

Preparing a meal

Indian Police Escort

Jordan's trading post, 1893

*A mock attack on the Rosebud
agency stockade, July 4th, 1897*

The Rosebud Sioux who were
with Buffalo Bill Cody's Wildwest
Show in 1890

Nellie Good Shield, circa 1889

Six Sons of Chief Iron Shell

*Four generations of Two Strike
family, 1914*

Tipis of the Chiefs, 4th of July, 1911

Cattle roundup for beef issue, 1902

Cattle to be issued, circa 1889

Beef day at Cut Meat, 1893

Women washing beef entrails in the creek

*Women preparing rawhide for a
shallow bowl*

COOKIN MEAT IN SKINS WITH HEATED STONES   COPYRIGHT 1911 BY J.A.ANDERSON.

*High Bear cooking by throwing
heated stones in beef-stomach
container*

Nº 267. INDIAN CELEBRATION.
PHOTO BY J. A. ANDRSON.

The Crook Treaty hitch lot, 1889

The White-Buffalo Ceremony, 1892

*Chief High Hawk's ceremonial
tipi with Winter Count, 1895*

A ceremonial tipi

Fool Bull a Medicine Man

Sun Dance, 1910

Carrying a child in a blanket

Old Bear Dog, son of Chief Iron Shell

Kills Two, a Brule Medicine Man, doing the "Big Missouri Winter Count" 1796-1926

The travois

He Dog and his wife, 1889

Eagle Man, a Medicine Man

Chief Iron Shell, 1900

Rosebud Home

Sioux Sportsmen, 1902

Yellow Hair and his wife, Plenty Horse

Good Voice Eagle, 1911

One Star

Goes to War, also called Pretty Bird, brother of Hollow Horn Bear

Sarah Blue Eyes, circa 1900

Red Feather and Father Buechel

Eugene Buechel, S.J.

was born in Schleida of Thuringia in Germany on October 20, 1874.
He received his early schooling in Fulda, Germany, from 1881-1897.
Buechel entered the Society of Jesus in Blyenback, Holland, in
1897 and came to the United States in 1900 to finish his Jesuit training.
He first arrived on the Rosebud as a young Jesuit teacher at St. Francis
Mission in 1902, and there is evidence that he made his first
photographs with an 8x10 viewcamera in these teaching years from
1902-1905. It is tempting to imagine what influence the successful
work of John Anderson, only a few miles away in Rosebud, might have
had on the beginning photographer. After his teaching assignment,
Buechel undertook theology studies in St. Louis and was ordained to
the Jesuit priesthood in 1906. His first assignment after ordination was
to Holy Rosary Mission on the Pine Ridge Reservation, where he
served as superior until 1916.

Fr. Buechel returned to St. Francis and Rosebud country in 1916
and was superior of the Mission until 1923. It was at this time that his
most ambitious photographic work began. He recorded exposures
made with a Folding Kodak No. 3 camera, carefully numbered the
negatives and prints, and identified the persons and places included in

the photographs. The first entry in his photo diary is dated August 14, 1922. His last exposure in the series, numbered 2128, was recorded on October 13, 1945. Numerous photographs, made during his time as superior and later as a pastor traveling to the isolated Indian communities on the Rosebud, were presented as gifts to the people he photographed or to benefactors interested in the work of the Mission. His small group portraits and candid snapshots include the families and activities of a variety of outlying Rosebud communities, many of which remained little affected by the new ways of reservation life.

Fr. Buechel's activities, however, were not concentrated around the work of photography. His pastoral duties absorbed most of his time and interest. His free time was also given to study of the Lakota Sioux language in which he was proficient. His 30,000 vocabulary cards were the first written documents of the Lakota language and provide the definitive reference even today for study of Lakota. He also carefully preserved specimens of the flora of the upper plains in all four seasons with identification in English, Latin, and Lakota. In addition, he was given a large collection of native Sioux artifacts. On his 50th anniversary as a Jesuit in 1947 a museum was constructed in St. Francis to display his precious collection of native Sioux culture. Fr. Buechel's photographic negatives, prints, and diaries were added to the archives of the Buechel Memorial Lakota Museum in 1972. Prints from the collection have been shown on the reservation, in galleries across the country, and at the Museum of Modern Art in New York.

Fr. Buechel's later years were spent as pastor and in visiting his many old friends around the Mission. He continued his study of the Lakota language and his interest in native culture. He suffered a stroke in 1954 and died on October 27th at the age of 80. He was deeply mourned by a large number of Sioux friends, many of whom speak affectionately of him still today.

Mrs. Plenty Bull's place (5-23-31)

Arthur White Feather & his wife
Nellie Running on their wedding
day (9-15-29)

Mrs. Frank Four Horses with quilt

Theodore Bald Eagle & wife
Luella Williams (9-21-45)

Dance Hall and Camp at Norris,
Armistice Day (11-11-30)

*Mrs. Winnie Red Bird & daughter,
Mary Sue (7-4-42)*

Cooking a meal at Spring Creek

Sam Spotted War Bonnet after an accident (2-26-30)

Mercy Eagle Feather (9-15-41)

BE IT ENACTED BY THE SENATE AND HOUSE OF REPRESENTATIVES OF THE UNITED STATES OF AMERICA IN CONGRESS ASSEMBLED, That all non-citizen Indians born within the territorial limits of the United States be, and they are hereby, declared to be citizens of the United States: PROVIDED, That the granting of such citizenship shall not in any manner impair or otherwise affect the right of any Indian to tribal or other property.

Approved June 2, 1924

(Back row) Susie (Bear Shield)
and Joe Kills in Sight, Alice Boyle,
Charles Swift, Joe White Hat,
Viola Manning, Charlie Kills in
Sight, Amelia Schaffer, Jennie
(Hollow Horn Bear) Swift.

(Front row) Isidore and Justin
White Hat, Dorothy and Mercy
Little, Viola Walking Eagle, Pearl
Walking Eagle, Lorraine White
Hat, Chris Kills in Sight, Jonas
Swift. (8-18-30)

Rosie (Guerue) Hunts Horses
(7-4-42)

*Preparing Easter dinner at Upper
Cutmeat (4-19-30)*

Old Black Crow in Indian costume
(4-22-33)

Alfred Walking Eagle's boy in Indian costume (6-10-36)

Joe Understanding Crow and
Melissa Holy Eagle on day of
marriage (4-27-30)

*Viola Manning with Viola
Walking Eagle (8-18-30)*

Josephine Jumping Eagle in
airplane (9-21-28)

The Indian is expected to grasp in a couple of generations what the white man learned only after centuries.

Eugene Buechel, S.J.

John Cordier's big girl (6-14-32)

Leo Sharp Fish's three smallest children (9-11-31)

John Little Bald Eagle and three
boys at He Dog's Camp
(6-14-41)

Easter dinner in front of Cutmeat
Church (4-20-30)

(Back row) Pearl (White Hat) Walking Eagle holding son Harvey and her parents, Emily (Hollow Horn Bear) White Hat and Joseph White Hat

(Front row) Bernard and Albert White Hat, sons of Emily and Joseph. Emily White Hat was the youngest daughter of Chief Hollow Horn Bear (6-10-42)

H is path to the white man's standards, which he must now attain, is beset with tremendous difficulties. We ought to appreciate them.

Eugene Buechel, S.J.

Mr. & Mrs. Makes Noise in the
Woods (10-7-22)

Sun Dance at Rosebud in 1928
(9-20-28)

*Omaha Dance at Rosebud, a
clown between two dancers
(9-21-28)*

Mother General Aloysia &
Indians (5-1-31)

Moses Bulltail & wife in Indian regalia (9-28-31)

There is no doubt but that in time he will be as well educated as his brother, the white man — if he is given an equal chance.

Eugene Buechel, S.J.

Lucy Goes Among & children
with Levi Quick Bear (7-25-24)

*Spring Creek Church & Campers
on Memorial Day (5-30-37)*

Pearl Sangreau (5-28-28)

Bad Lands North of Charles Rooks

Isaac Crow & wife Jennie (Kills at Lodge) & baby Placides (12-26-27)

The whole Night Chase Family
(7-8-31)

Joe Fire Heart and his two horses
(4-15-39)

Ray Whipple pulling Fr. Buechel's
car (3-4-33)

It is quite natural, too, that the white man's way of life had no appeal for the Indian. It takes more than a couple of generations to absorb a new philosophy, a new economy. It would have been easier for the Indian if the white man had not taken the good land and left him only arid, dusty acres from which no man could earn a living. Living on a lower standard than he did when the forests and plains were rich in game, the red man became a victim of many diseases.

Eugene Buechel, S.J.

Sam Spotted War Bonnet & family
(10-16-29)

Group of six girls (11/26)

Winnie Iyott and baby

Spring Creek on Memorial Day

Bessie Moccasin Face's funeral
(4-30-23)

Don Doll, S.J.

was born July 15, 1937, in Milwaukee, Wisconsin. He attended primary and secondary schools in Milwaukee and after graduation entered the Jesuit novitiate in September, 1955. His early Jesuit education took place at St. Louis University where he earned degrees in philosophy and education. It was not until he was assigned to St. Francis Mission as a young Jesuit that Doll, like Fr. Buechel, began working with a camera. While teaching, coaching, and supervising the boys' dormitory, he began making photographs with his students for the school's publications. His apprenticeship was done with make-shift equipment and self-instruction during limited free time. It was, however, during these years that he made the lasting acquaintances of the Sioux students and parents that remain intimate with him today. In 1964 he received his first formal instruction at Marquette University in photojournalism and it was at this time that his photographic avocation became a vocation. He left the Rosebud Reservation in 1965 to continue theology studies at St. Mary's, Kansas, and later at St. Louis University. He was ordained a Jesuit priest in 1968 and was appointed to the faculty of Creighton University in

Omaha, Nebraska, as an instructor of photography in 1969.

Fr. Doll has studied photography since 1965 and attended various workshops and professional sessions at the University of Oregon, the University of Missouri, and Santa Clara University. His acquaintances with the Rosebud people, especially in the reservation community of Spring Creek, have been deepened since 1965 by repeated visits. The combination of his friendship, pastoral concern, and appreciation of the natural beauty and style of life in Spring Creek contributed to his acceptance in Spring Creek as one of the community. During one stay with the people he was given the Indian name *Wahacankayapi,* which translates "He Who Shields Him" because, as one of the patriarchs of the village said, "We feel safe when you are in town."

In 1974, Fr. Doll arranged to spend one year on leave from Creighton to live in Spring Creek as the parish priest and to photograph in the community. His purpose was to portray the residents in their environment and to promote an understanding of Indian life on the reservation. The result of this work was a series of over 100 images representing the land, the people, and the quality of life in Spring Creek. The photographs were first shown in Spring Creek. In September, 1975, the show opened at Creighton. In April of 1976 Fr. Doll received "special recognition" in the World Understanding category of the Pictures of the Year Competition.

Fr. Doll is presently chairman of the Fine and Performing Arts Department at Creighton University where he continues camerawork and teaching photography.

Road to Spring Creek

Sewel Makes Room for Them

Spring Creek, South Dakota is a typical reservation town with a population of 175 full-blood Brule Sioux — many of whom are much more comfortable speaking their native Lakota language than English.

About thirty homes nestle in the Little White River valley, surrounded by hills covered with Ponderosa pine. The prairie stretches thirty to forty miles west and south without a tree to obstruct vision. Spring Creek has no gas station and no grocery store. The employer in town is the Spring Creek Grade School which hires Indians as teacher aides. Shopping is done in Valentine, Nebraska, forty-five miles to the southeast. About sixty per cent of the people in Spring Creek have access to a car. There is, of course, no public transportation. The road ends in Spring Creek.

Vision is cleared by the reservation's empty sky. Discarded *uwipi* (medicine) bundles, left behind from someone's vision quest, are reminders that the trails, the rolling hills, the land once belonged to them. The "People." A direct question about the Indian's relation to the land will not be answered; it never is in Indian cultures. Observation and clear vision must suffice.

Don Doll, S.J.

Anna Rose White Hat, with
Tyrone, Camille, Marlon and J.J.

Rosebud Reservation

Billy and Mervin Marshall

Gordon Swift Hawk

Victor Makes Room for Them,
deer hunting along the Little
White River

Martin and Victor Makes Room for Them led the Spring Creek Singers. Everyone knew the Spring Creekers by their high-pitched and distinctive sound. The incessant beat of the drummers and the wailing of the singers cuts through the crowd.

Black Elk's often quoted prayer is, "that the people may live." The beat of the drum is the pulse of the people—an affirmation that life goes on.

Don Doll, S.J.

*Martin & Victor Makes Room for
Them and Spring Creek Singers*

Charles Kills in Water on his 83rd birthday.

Louie and Lillian Walking Eagle
with Cornell

Orville and Ophelia Kills in Sight,
with Junior

Cleveland Kills in Sight with
Kenny, Raymond, Samuel,
Bernadine, and Bernadette

Noah and Emily are perhaps my closest friends in Spring Creek. I don't think this photograph portrays their personalities well. However, I do think it is a good photograph/metaphor/symbol to convey what has happened to the Indian people. I don't know where the sadness on their faces came from. I think they are reacting to me.

When I made this photograph I could have cried for what the people suffer. Somehow, I feel that Noah and Emily had sensed this.

Don Doll, S.J.

Noah and Emily Kills in Sight

Stanley Redbird

Ernestine Makes Room for Them

Sewel, Frank, Gladys Makes
Room for Them, Linda Forgets
Nothing, Twila Makes Room for
Them, and Elmer Bravebird

(back row) Dominic, Junior and
Willard Makes Room for Them
(front row)

Daniel White Hat and Nellie Little

Leo holds Rocky whose jaw was swollen for two days. It was hard for Victor and Sherry to take him to the Rosebud Service Unit Hospital 20 miles away because they had no car. They couldn't call for help either; only 10 per cent of Indian homes have phones. At the hospital out-patients wait three to four hours for treatment from a staff rated at half strength. Less than one-fifth of Indian three-year-olds get complete immunization. Indian children die at 3 times the national average.

Don Doll, S.J.

Leo Makes Room for Them, with Rocky

Jack Menards and Linda Rose Kills
in Sight's month old daughter

Caroline Kills in Water, age 87

*Saturday afternoon: Kenny Kills
in Sight, Wendell White Eyes,
"Yogi Bear" Left Hand Bull,
Rafael Kills in Sight, and Brian
Left Hand Bull*

Morris Kills in Sight, Glenford
Walking Eagle, Ambrose, Sylvan
and Daniel White Hat

Three hundred seventy-five "transitional" houses were built in 21 communities on the reservation in 1966 through a cooperative effort of the Rosebud Sioux tribe, OEO, HUD, BIA and PHS. Spring Creek received 27. Each was designed to be heated by one stove, either wood or oil. The people were to pay $5.00 a month for three years to a local home improvement association; after three years a title to the house would be granted.

The houses were called transitional because they were considered a transition from disaster to some kind of minimum standards.

The people preferred them to the more modern "Sioux 400's" which came later and required as much as $100 a month in propane for heating during the Dakota winters.

Mrs. Corrine Cloudman's
"Transitional" home

Interior of Corrine Cloudman's home

Spring Creek, South Dakota

Sherry Makes Room for Them,
giving Rocky a bath

Victor Makes Room for Them

Interior of Julia Kills in Sight's
home

Along the Little White River

Average annual income for families on the Rosebud Reservation is $3,500 or $760 per capita. Half of this is earned income and half unearned coming from lease receipts and public assistance. At times unemployment in Spring Creek runs as high as 80 to 90 per cent. Only two families in Spring Creek do not qualify to receive commodity foods through the United States Department of Agriculture. Individuals earning over $183 per month or families of five receiving over $368 per month are excluded. More than 5,000 of the 8,000 people living at Rosebud qualify.

Summarized from the Public Health Service Report (1975); and a personal interview with Dallas Walking Eagle, Director, United States Department of Agriculture Commodoties Office at Rosebud.

In July, 1976 each family of five received:

dry beans 3 two lb. bags	all purpose flour 10 five lb. bags	orange juice 5 one qt. cans
rolled oats 3 two lb. bags	margarine 10 one lb. packages	purple plums 5 29 oz. cans
corn meal 3 five lb. bags	chicken 5 29 oz. cans	prunes 5 one lb. bags
peanut butter 2 two lb. cans	beef 5 20 oz. cans	farina (cereal) 5 14 oz. boxes
dry milk 2 four lb. boxes	egg mix 5 16 oz. packages	instant potatoes 5 one lb. bags
cheese 2 five lb. boxes	green beans 5 16 oz. cans	apple juice 5 one qt. cans
shortening 2 three lb. cans	macaroni 5 one lb. packages	grapefruit juice 5 one qt. cans
evaporated milk 30 14 oz. cans	syrup 5 one pt. jars	

Interior of Peter Swift Hawk's
home

Eleanor Kills in Sight on her first
Communion day

Morris Kills in Sight

High school graduation brings both a happy and a sad day. Happy because it is an achievement that parents are proud of — only one-third of the students who start high school finish. It is sad because the future probably will be bleak. Although there is government funding for Indian higher education only 23 per cent of Rosebud high school graduates take advantage of it. In 1975 according to the Bureau of Indian Affairs, $32,956,000 was granted to 14,700 Indian students across the nation. Each received an average of $1,750. In the same year 850 Indian students were graduated from colleges out of a freshman class that initially numbered 3,500.

On the reservation there is little to do; but there is so much to forget. Because of the drinking, almost everyone has experienced tragedy, often at a very young age. To forget, one drinks. But when one drinks, one is liable to do something else that he will regret when he sobers up. He can live with that for awhile feeling miserable about himself — until he can take it no longer, and drinks again to forget. And so the circle does not end.

Don Doll, S.J.

Graduation

Memorial Day, 1974

Julia Walking Eagle at husband
Abel's grave, Memorial Day, 1974

When asked what he prayed, Abraham responded:

I pray for all the people.

Every time that I go to the cemetery, I pray before
      the crucifix.

I pray that they may have strength and find peace.

I pray with many words.

I am sure that God hears at least one of them.

Abraham Kills in Sight

The 'give-away' is a misnomer. It really is a sharing and a remembering of the deceased person. It's a way of beginning over again. You put the past behind you and start over.

Fr. Noah Broken Leg
Episcopal priest for Spring Creek

Pearl Walking Eagle's "Give-
away" in honor of her husband
Harvey on day of funeral

Harvey Walking Eagle's son
Freddy with Harvey's Bronze Star
from World War II

Team and Wagon leading procession in Harvey Walking Eagle's funeral